IMAGINAR
REPUBLICS
Poems 1984–1993

OTHER WORKS BY WILLIAM BEDFORD

POETRY

Whatever There Is Of Light (The Mandeville Press, 1975)

The Hollow Landscapes (Hippopotamus Press, 1977)

Journeys (Agenda Editions, 1988)

FICTION

Happiland (Heinemann, 1990; Mandarin, 1991)

*The Golden Gallopers** (The Bodley Head, 1991)

All Shook Up (Macmillan, 1992; Picador, 1993)

*Nightworld** (The Bodley Head, 1992)

Catwalking (Macmillan, 1993; Picador, 1994)

* *for children*

IMAGINARY REPUBLICS
Poems 1984–1993

by
William Bedford

LOXWOOD STONELEIGH
BRISTOL

First published by Loxwood Stoneleigh in 1993

Copyright © 1993 William Bedford

Designed and typeset by Falling Wall Press Ltd, Bristol
Printed and bound in Great Britain by BPCC Wheatons Ltd, Exeter
Cover printed by Doveton Press Ltd, Bristol

British Library Cataloguing-in-Publication Data
A catalogue record for this book is available from the British Library.

ISBN 1 85135 018 7

Loxwood Stoneleigh
11 Colston Yard, Colston Street, Bristol BS1 5BD, England

For William Cookson

Contents

Acknowledgements are due to the editors of the following magazines in which versions of some of these poems originally appeared: *Acumen, Agenda, Ariel, Contrasts, Creative Language, Encounter, The Malahat Review, Oasis, Outposts, Pennine Platform, Poetry Durham, Washington Times* and *Verse*.

W.B.

Night Watching

All night you cry in your cradle,
and *What to do with the child*
becomes the heat's chorus,
hanging on the edge of darkness
like a bat winging from the chimney,
slamming at our frayed control.

We argue, walk about, listen.
In your cradle, your tears echo:
'*What to do with the child*
will become your Greek chorus;
you will sing it with wild eyes;
spend hours arguing and forgiving.'

In the trees, the bat knows better:
hangs from leaves; ignores us;
glistens.
                    At dawn, I open a window.
The milkman rattles the path alive.
Light swims across the geraniums.
An owl, screeching, passes.

All night, you keep us awake,
then sleep with your fists clenched,
your tiny hands frozen.
I make tea and go out into the garden.
A goldfinch hops from the gate.
French marigolds lick the sun.

Down the lane, traffic dazzles silence.
I wait for you to cry. I wait.
And in years to come,
I'll remember this disturbed morning,
the chaffinch carrying winter's flashes,
dust snowing on a bat's grave.

We will no longer argue,
the man and woman pacing in a hot room,
the full moon sinking in its wild flight.
We will be separated by what held us.
And you will have your own child,
my grandchild to make me feel older,

to smile at me with my own smile.
Perhaps I will show her French marigolds,
geraniums like a pool of water.
We will laugh at the young milkman,
struggling with the garden gate;
the sun, in full flight, passing.

Somersby

The church squats like a grey toad,
huddled on the escarpment's edge,
waiting for a mighty claw from heaven.
When we open the door, the cold hurts:

black pews and a blacker heaven
hidden among yews and leaking stones;
the hollow eye of the collecting bowl.
But that voice crying 'Father, forgive them',

is the wind, surely, in the ugly tower,
guilt singing its familiar blackmail?
We stand, rigid, in the empty porch,
words raining from coloured glass,

pain leaping from the saintly histories.
In leafless branches, ghosts weep,
children of our soiled imagination:
the taut farmers and parish councillors,

angry women with their sullen lives.
Outside, in sun, the yews creak.
The sundial spreads its green corrosion.
Through frozen hedgerows, time leaks.

After the War

(i.m. Annie Elizabeth Bodsworth, died 1st November 1927)

Walking the field on a winter morning,
you know that singling sugar-beet is hard,
another year of crow-scaring and harvest
like sheaves of cold metal round your heart.
You know the steady ache of loss not healing,
the round of plodding days on carrier's cart.
And yet you sing: lead kindly light and songs
of morning broken, his crystal wireless
humming in your mind, his auburn hair
your one, unfading token. Is such grief kind?
These frozen furrows lead me to your grave,
the bitter group that stood bare-headed mourners
silent where the hawthorn berries grow,
their reddening glow your wild winter morning.

The Beck

(For my father)

You must have played beside this beck,
crossing the cold flood on market days
or cutting down the hawthorns lovers use,
the dog rose hips for wilder autumn brew.
Did water dazzle soul beside that stream,
crow-scaring and church the nightmare dream
that woke you to the sullen trap of school,
your restless eyes on sunlit open fields,
your mind an afternoon of games away?
Some teacher must have called you fool.
You never took to books, ignored their fame.
Your smile was harvests, children's random play.
You gave me berries, gathered from the weed,
forget-me-nots to light this sudden need.

Inside the Glasshouse

Obliquely,
I question nurserymen,
and their answers come roughly,

like a new crop,
forced through the black earth.
Their eyes search for honesty.

I have entered
like a threat of rain,
cold on their shuttered doors,

my words
stunning their animosity.
Their hands work through it all,

their eyes
fixed on the soil,
their voices mastering heat.

Outside, the sun yields:
a movement towards October,
a freshening in the bright sky.

Inside, the heat continues:
clinging like a damp sheet,
breeding a vast oblivion.

Film Sequence

Looking across a room,
your smile touched me like a glance
in an Italian film,
welcoming the handsome stranger.
At first, I thought it was someone else,
an old acquaintance, or a dreamer,
perhaps, of love, broken by a casual kiss.
When you spoke I knew the film was true.

And that summer, the days spreading out
from cut to gentle cut,
we played each scene with a calm
that amazed our friends,
a love affair of statuettes and fountains.
The critics, unaware,
discussed our passion, as fading August
wrapped us in despair.

And yet your going was an act
I'd not imagined,
abrupt departure altering the play,
an ending I had somehow overlooked.
Protective, all our friends are now divided,
our separation casual as a kiss,
acquaintances, or images of love.
And we alone have nothing left to say.

Recluse

In a landscape of white and speckled shells,
your voice insists upon wordless patterns,
the sea crashing tides of sunlight,
the mysteries ignored
that sink and vaguely multiply.

The sea isolates your dreams:
old memories of love and conversation,
photographs and wrecks of forgotten tenderness.
Somewhere, there are girls' voices,
losing their natural kindness,

and the sound of rehearsed laughter,
spreading in the dark like waves.
Your thoughts congregate in silence,
protected from life and death,
as your ease supports all forgiveness.

In the rooms where we first met,
we pause to remember your beginning,
that night of cigarettes and stars
when you found your strange uniqueness,
the pose that we all admired.

Then, we imagined your insanity:
a slow tightening of the brain surging towards
the moon, a bleak absence of light.
Your voice is obscured by the distance.
The pain, black guillemot, is ours.

Outsider

Evenings are what you remember best,
when trees can be graceful
and conversation
                              move quietly to silence,
surrounded by summer darkness.
Then, you are safe in your dreams,
a world understood,
a gentle comprehension.

As a child, you seek protection,
flowers and droning fields,
a shield of distance
                              to calm the loud hours.
Outside, I note your preparations:
journeys begun, smiles leading to silence,
the careful words
that open, then conceal.

But finally, your kindness is a barrier,
innocence we observe,
laughter
                              we use as ritual.
Outside, I remain the audience,
and trapped like strangers,
we talk of fields and flowers,
noticing their quiet preparation.

Aware Continuously

Aware continuously of the silence
that moves between us,
you pour a drink,
place records with precise care,
and take that stance
which hides your true feelings.

                                In my chair,
I finger glass,
the slow, transparent moments
drifting to a close,
the record ending as the needle lifts.

End of Season

When I arrive, this end of season silence
        holds me,
like the walls containing tides,
a tall exposure of melancholy.
All morning, I search among shadows,
the eyeless shops, the green stare of shutters,
the streets winding into water.
Blind with a fine sand,
October lurches towards me,
a sandcrab pincered motion, chased by a circling dog.

The event, as always, escapes description.
        I see your smile,
ghosting a desolate seashore,
the dog and gull chased hours leading to the sea,
the misery of half remember memories.
What's left of pain lingers in the eyes,
and the sea empties into sky,
draining a tired emotion.
Enormous, the past surrounds me,
like a graveyard of summer's laughter.

Yet the town is not prepared for my questions.
        Wrapped in bright colours,
tarted by paint and lighting, it heaves
reluctantly into winter, ignoring the summer's end
in a brief, electric charade.
For a month, the old are welcome,
and the sick, led by their nurses, staring at the promenade.
Cheap rates and fog for October,
and a wind, cutting to the heart,
reminding them of things they had forgotten.

In chairs, they move towards silence.
        Their smiles are rehearsed,
their eyes dulled with expectation,
their hands, gripping and relaxing.
Alone, or travelling in pairs,
they trundle bleakly through the morning,
all laughter exaggeration,
their voices wavering in the air.
As usual, the town is prepared,
and sweeps them gaily into battalions,

cheap rates and empty hotels.
        Going by me,
they ignore my stare, indifferent
as the shells and your memory.
The event, as always, escapes description,
and I pincer, like the sandcrab, into silence,
turning from the mournful shores.
To this, our love will take us,
the knowledge that loneliness clarifies,
the escape from loss into tedium.

The Floods

'There have been other floods and other losses'
          your letter seemed to imply,
but your grief eddies around us, like the dross
caught up by fishermen, brought in on a dawn tide.
Without you, we return to see the ruin,
preparing for the pain we have to share.
And here, there are no shadows to deceive:
the broken pier, the rust and drowning mud,
the promenade a flattened, desolate mile,
all indicate the loss your words conceal.

Amusement, like a joke, grins from its awnings,
          where tattered signs hang useless
in the sun, and loud arcades and palaces of fun
seem almost catastrophic with their warnings,
the preacher's voice a hell-fire in the wind.
A broken jetty reaches to the sea,
like fingers of a hand spread out and blackening,
and we are left with emptiness and dark,
a seagull crying bleakly in the sky
as foghorns mourn the need we have to die.

Unspeaking, through disaster, we explore,
          like visitors with ticket
and brochure, our silent course through
other people's lives a brief despair
that fades, and then revives.
Without you, lugworms pock the empty shores,
regardless of the latest absences,
deserted grave of junk and beachcombers.
And here the weed, and here the silence spread,
as gulls disgorge the memory of the dead.

Here winter held the moment of your grief,
        the life you lived, the hopes
you gave expression, the walls against unmeaning
that we build, with wives and friends
and families, those temporary obsessions.
A silence lies unmoving round your loss,
and all we are, and all we dreamed, seems hopeless,
the meaning, like a firework, turning stars,
until the end displays its lack of purpose,
until the time for suffering is ours.

And so you come, your letter finally answered,
        the details met, the buried
left behind, the necessary papers neatly signed,
and we are left to try and find an answer.
No words we utter break the soundless tide:
a gaiety, a brightness of intent,
a silly humour spoiled by what it meant,
mean nothing in the face of such despair.
Your words, unspoken, silent as the stone:
we have no meaning beyond the things we own.

But finally, you take us back to grief,
        as if expecting time
to change the scene, providing answers solitude
can't find. A crying bittern booms
across the sky, a wintry sun evaporates your dreams.
And tiding on a wash of mournful gulls,
your stillness, like the dawn, must meet the sea,
as winter coastlines meet extremity.
Our understanding measures what we are,
our knowledge, in the end, what we can bear.

Grenville Place

(For Fakhry Kostandi)

1. CLEARING YOUR ROOM

You were my friend, Fakhry Kostandi,
and clearing your room this winter morning
I find the fungus of forgotten meals,
pushed under the bed like the Brecht
you annotated, the rind of orange peel.
Hard frost grows on the attic windows,
and the smell of sour Turkish coffee
sweetens the air of a July evening
where the St. Pancras Players applaud
their applauding audience, and the pigeons
mob the trees on Onslow Square. 1964:
summer of *Szechwan* and the Beatles,
my marriage and your Ph.D.,
then the long journey back to Cairo.

2. AUGUST 1963

From heat and dust I salvage August,
old newsreel facades my madeleine:
loud music rising from the stalled traffic,
women, wet lipped, on the underground.
In the room below, the nightly typewriter,
and somebody nearer playing a guitar –
that Chinese student studying music,
or the Persian girl on the ground floor
who smiles when I collect my letters,
answer the telephone outside her door.
You visit my room with Turkish coffee,
faded photographs of a Cairo bazaar.
We talk, all night, about Walter Benjamin,
and walk in Kensington Gardens at dawn.

3. GHOSTS

The years Prufrock slept in these rooms
there were maples growing in select squares
and brilliant women down cobbled mews,
talking politics and 78s,
dressing from *Harpers* for Fred Astaire.
Now Madonna lives in the rooms below,
with her video films and sleeping pills,
shrieking with laughter at the latest *Vogue*,
maudlin with lust over cinema stills.
On a drunken night, we ate laburnum,
risking poison in a noisy square
where Prufrock chattered like a mad monkey
and pigeons squabbled above the trees,
sad drunken pilots playing solitaire.

4. STILL LIFE

Your yellow wallpaper and canvas chair
brush their pale textures against the dawn.
On a shelf, your mirror reflects the wall,
inches of toothpaste, like a snail's spoor.
At eleven, you say you are going to leave.
But neither of us moves: you slip idly
through second-hand words, fingering *Life
Studies* and pretending to read.
I imagine you, dancing in blue clothes . . .
while outside the traffic pumps monoxide,
a grinding of streets round our rented room,
black-headed gulls like a flock of nightmares.
At the window, you mock my old turmoil,
smiling as you turn to leave: your new pose.

5. POETRY SOCIETY

When Lennon lived in Emperor's Gate
fans carved their lust on his blue door
and Prufrock's ghost was forced to wait,
baffled by the music and Rolls Royce
that spoiled his early morning communion.
Now Lennon's ghost has a Brooklyn haunt,
and T.S. Eliot springs alive
with annual volumes the pleased critics
declare 'okay' though 'unauthorised.'
A Concord sings over Earls Court Square,
and Boy George fans now congregate
wherever the loudest volumes slam,
like scented talcum, their scented brains.
A tenant sold the door in Emperor's Gate.

6. WINTER 1964

My London grind of ice and traffic
freezes to this sludge of music and snow,
the memories you indict without humour:
Salah u Din, my friend, clapping –
the German teacher stripping her clothes,
dancing, high-heeled, on a kitchen table –
that student downstairs playing her records.
The sound of their laughter crept in our lives,
her German vowels in the ruined plumbing,
his antique politeness, nervous prose.
You sat all night by a shuttered window,
reading Spinoza in the desolate light.
High-heeled, on somebody else's table,
dark frauleins move through my winter dreams.

7. GRENVILLE PLACE

Play me Miles Davis's *Kind of Blue*,
black coffee music for this midnight hour
when the drunks swim along Cromwell Road
and police in pandas radio the moon.
The rooms are quiet where Prufrock lay,
Italian Dante to keep him warm.
On darkened landings the wind sighs
and desolate women stand alone.
Dawn is coming, with its empty parks.
The daylight will tell us what to do.
But for the time being, lonely heart,
play me Miles Davis's *Kind of Blue*,
these new rumours of the awful night
holding us closely, as lovers do.

The Suicide

'One day, in the autumn of 1845, I accidentally lighted on a MS
volume of verse in my sister Emily's handwriting.'

Charlotte Bronte

You read my poems in manuscript,
wounding that secret, inward eye
nothing forgets, nothing forgives.

Now black on moors, a snowing sky,
your figure shuffles at the frost
as though you'd force me not to die,

searching for the heather I lost,
your heart aching at what's given,
your tears mourning the brutal cost.

Yet you read what I had wished hidden:
a soul broken, a spirit's grief,
a frenzy over wild snow driven,

wounding that secret, inward eye
nothing forgets, nothing forgives,
leaving no freedom except to die.

Heathcliffe

(An old slave woman remembers her first owner in Trinidad)

They say he was mad with love.
Drank to forget. Raged at the moon.
Brooded like a dark, religious dove.

Sand, wildly, and out of tune.
I never saw a white dove black.
Our weeping years made his fortune.

Was he the one with the bruised back?
He came, once, to my small room,
stood in the door, his mouth slack,

his eyes shining their frantic doom,
his hands twitching at his side.
Our weeping hours made his fortune.

Our misery was his pride.
He woke, late, in the hot night.
I felt his terror deep inside,

his eyes yellow, sick with fright.
He called my name, and it was my name:
Cathy, Cathy, to the moon's flight.

When he left me, I felt the pain,
the child, waiting, solemnly move,
the steady fall of summer rain.

They say he was mad with love.
Drank to forget. Raged at the moon.
Brooded like a dark, religious dove.

Sang, wildly, and out of tune.
I never saw a white dove black.
Our weeping years made his fortune.

Family Picnic on the East Coast: 1982

(i.m. Kenneth Bratton, died 31st July 1982)

'Captain Roberts, anxious about the low clouds gathering on the
horizon to the west, took a large telescope and asked permission to
climb the lighthouse, where he watched the sails of the *Don Juan*
until they disappeared into a thickening haze.'

Richard Holmes

1.

You walk the marram dunes on your own,
imagining our picnic's in Byron's honour,
a promise kept with your student days
of revolution, always revolution.
A circus passes on the coast road.
Children sing in vans. A driver waves.
The decorations shine in brilliant sun.
And that's what being young now means:
the traffic all night south across a bridge,
the yellow river red with dawn sun.
You face the sea, a saltmarsh, desolate estuary,
a strandline scavenged clean by sanderling.
Here nothing shapes the day, nothing dreams,
the shallow sea fulfilling your cold will.

2.

But emptying the wine,
I link arms with our old professor
and walk through Shelley's final day:
the small boat tiding into thickening haze,
two women standing at a harbour window.
It is the ghosts of children make that noise,
clattering among vines, running to the sea.
Listen to the voices: they are our children,
who dream of circuses every day,
an estuary alive with blue seiners,
factories on the widening river bend.
'I read, much of the night, and go south in the winter.'
But that was another day. And revolution,
revolution, the Gulf of Spezia our bright fresh day.

The Last Red Squirrel

(For Thomas)

The cows at pasture
steam from a wet light
as though somebody's hand
had painted them on the meadow,

munching at grass,
crushing the soft buttercups.
That buttercup meadow
is all you remember,

not the last red squirrel,
leaping out of elms
like a clown
throwing dust in our eyes,

cartwheeling
over cows as if they were questions
left out to be answered,
history books where all the talk is of squirrels.

To Tell You the Truth

(Barcelona: 1968)

I guess I'm faking anguish
to get this essay in metaphor,
a grand way of saying thank you

when all that's needed is a wave
and a baked, absolute light
like the hills around Barcelona,

the ground thick with pine-cones,
the tracks leading up into snow.
It was there we met a birdcatcher,

sitting under the trees
with a homemade wooden cage,
imitating the song of a woodpecker.

I told him there was no market
for woodpeckers, but you insisted
we should leave him alone,

get on with our own lives.
I never forgot the birdcatcher.
You, walking beneath pines.

And the baked, absolute tremor
of heat scorching your face,
happiness, widening in your eyes.

Letter from Cumbria

'We boast our light; but if we look not wisely on the sun itself, it
smites us into darkness.'

Milton

The sky has dropped. I guess you know.
White dust scatters on forest pine.
A brilliant sunlight scalds the snow.

Will there be loud arcades of time,
flowers to erupt their wild grace,
histories for us? You are mine.

I am yours. I know your face,
your hands, our children's blue eyes . . .
You not here, I whisper into space.

And daffadillies, Coleridge sighs,
growing quickly beside the lake,
leaping from the mirroring skies –

daffadillies melt and shake,
vibrating in the molten air.
Where poets cherished all they make,

these makers witness our despair,
ghosts waiting for the sun to slow.
Alone, I wonder where you are.

The sky has dropped. I guess you know.
White dust scatters on forest pine.
A brilliant sunlight scalds the snow.

Cities of the Plain

Protect us from the light on snow,
dazzling bright perfection
each of us must separately know.

Blackbirds call for our attention,
the calculating thrush
and quick arctic tern's direction

lead to winter's frozen ambush.
Bones in the desert dry.
Children burn in Abraham's bush.

I know the bittern's funeral cry.
We are born alone,
lonely, rent rooms in which to die.

I know the city streets have grown
a solitary ache,
a wind chill to the human bone.

Yet wisdom keeps the streets awake,
where the hurt heart must go,
lost in turmoil's darkening opaque.

Protect us from the light on snow,
dazzling bright perfection
each of us must separately know.

Winter Occupation

(USAF Hemswell: 1962)

Winter's light is brilliant,
blue on fields of snow;
guards flick their glasses
where native farmers plough.

The road at the perimeter,
open to deceive;
the tall wire enclosing
their military need.

Indifferent sheep grazing
nose to a frozen east;
a single car disrupts
our January peace.

Snowed-in, we hear voices,
chorus on the wind;
this necessary madness
to protect mankind.

Male and female citizens
read on frosted glass
news of fresh Hiroshimas
to help the hours pass.

And hear loud music,
solace for their youth,
popular and brazen,
cheap empires of truth.

The arc lamps at midnight
shine on pale eyes;
the snow ploughs stutter,
gathering tall skies,

as winter's light fractures,
blue on fields of snow;
guards flick their glasses
where native farmers plough.

The Redlit Boys

(For my mother)

'Through the open doors of foundries you see fiery serpents of iron
being hauled to and fro by redlit boys, and you hear the whizz and
thump of steam hammers and the scream of iron under the blow.'

George Orwell

1. THE REDLIT BOYS

The redlit boys explode in your dreams,
steam-hammering the snakes of fiery iron
that pour like white heat from furnace mouths,
clamouring *sin* between each screaming blow.
At four o'clock, you struggle out of bed,
and ride through Brightside on the dawn tram,
strap-hanging slide from Tinsley Depot
down as far as Wicker, "Peacock & Mullholland,"
where you collect the morning papers.
Your mother stands with papers at Firth Brown.
In time for school, you kick the cobbles home,
a red-haired twelve year old,
following the lamplighter's flint and hook,
breathing sulphur off the River Don,
your fiery eyes enough to break my heart.

2. SEEING YOU HOME

Acetylene flares outside the shops
glare into the brick, Attercliffe dawn,
a choir of angels flung from melted frost.
You blow white air to keep your hands warm,
stamp your feet, and chase a rain of sparks
that hisses from the crackling blue cables.
At six 'o' clock, you sing the draymen home,
hurry your breakfast, light the first fire,
then sit beside the kitchen range and dream:
a River Don alive with young carp –
moors at the window, purpling in the heat –
your brothers scrambling tips of free slack.
I cannot see you home: ride the loud trams,
breathe on the coal; imagine you not alone,
the morning's papers stuffed beneath your arm.

3. STANDING

(For my grandmother)

She scorned the loafers who couldn't pay,
a week's money gone on watered beer,
their children's bellies clamouring for grub –
Mary Ellen Parnham at the works gate,
tobacco and news to start the fresh day.
Her hymns and sermons filled the sour air,
familiar tunes of guilt and promised lands,
their cunning mixture acid to men's coins.
She lost her eye running from a street brawl,
boys throwing stones in the gaslit cold –
met your father when he came to decorate,
their courting done in Fletcher's old van,
William and Mary, celebrating work.
I knew their warmer, kinder final years.
You felt the slap of hands too tired to love.

4. THE BREAD HORSE

You saw him home from Carbrook Primary,
his nose blooded in a ginnel brawl
with Arthur Cousins and Jeremiah Reed,
brothers yelling for a chance to kick
the only bread horse left in Dunlop Place.
You called their mother slag, ugly cow,
then ran for cover down by Carbrook Weir,
the Brightside Works yellow on black ice.
They only had one mother. Joe had no lunch,
the bread horse giving rides for relishes,
pigs' trotters, saveloys, dripping, cow heels,
lard sandwiches like doorsteps in the mouth.
They caught you, and donkey-stoned your cheek,
grazing the skin with slow, idiot smiles.
The bread horse joined the dole. Walked the streets.

5. JUBILEE

Jolf Moore showed you how to cut jubilee,
damming the stream from Tinsley Colliery
where the coal dust was washed off coal,
pumped out onto scrubby derelict land.
A layer of coal dust blocked the stream,
wet and compressed like freshly cut coal.
He said these black cubes were jubilee,
though nobody'd ever told him why.
He tried to hold your hand. Bought you flowers.
Trudged from the waste land with a barrow
made of packing cases, shoes tied up
with strings from his mother's aprons.
Stacked under their kitchen sink to dry,
the cubes whispered like roots of trees,
a singing forest washed from a cold stream.

6. BRICK FIELDS

Old ashes, rank elder, willow-herb –
the brick fields darken in evening sun,
surrounded by gas-works, factories, breweries,
the public urinals' reddening grime.
From the methodist chapel, music exhorts:
the drunks, the lovers, the child-abusers,
the backward child and rouged daughter.
In alleyways and courts, snickets and ginnels,
laughter welcomes the gap-toothed crime.
You never crossed brick fields alone.
On foggy days, gangs roamed in the dark,
their clinkered, six-acred battle-ground
surrounded by soot and industrial light,
the steel hammers threatening revolution,
the ragged trousers, shining and worn.

7. THE SIN EATER

Your cousin Winifred walked the moors,
leaving behind the straight tracks of trams
from Attercliffe to Crookesmoor Cemetery,
the furnace flames like pale dawn flowers.
She sought the ferned track. Stumbled
in winter sunlight through frozen snow.
Broke the thin mirror on pools of ice.
Bells from the churches welcomed her pain.
She found the buried sheep. Terns singing.
A frenzy of clouds boiling from Man Tor.
The crows she disturbed circled up above,
alarming the men who came to find her,
her long dress shreds of coloured ribbon,
her sleeping child alive in the cold womb.
God's eyes, alert, winked in the sudden sun.

8. MUSIC HALL

(For Queenie Storey)

You heard the evening tingle-aireys*
barrel-organ down the darkening streets,
brick dust and twilight your only music,
the rattle of milkbottles in cobbled streets,
red doorsteps shining in a drenched dawn.
When rag-and-bone men offered goldfish
for used jam jars and tattered clothes,
you heard the sound of your own music:
the gas flares of the lame lamplighter,
children scrambling for lumps of coal,
your father's shout in the dark road:
children should be seen and not listened to,
dirty miracles to be worked and belted.
You trod the music halls like a rare treat,
with your strange music of the tingle-aireys.

tingle-aireys: barrel organs

9. FETTLING*

(For my great-grandfather)

You sang like a foxglove on a dunghill
your grandson wrote, sending me stories
of poverty days, Brightside and Attercliffe
in gothic script you wouldn't recognise,
selling your pies and peas to pub drunks
and singing in that fine aggressive voice
last orders for the landlords of misery,
your cannisters of grub as cold as beer,
fists like steel you'd fettled at the works.
Your wife left you when you got too loud,
John Thomas Parnham, widowed by disgust.
You were foreman till Edgar Allen's closed,
when you took to riding a hired bike,
bouncing over cobbles glistening with rain,
black bullets for a dawn that won't arrive.

* *Fettling*: taking the rough edges off steel.

10. DANDELION AND BURDOCK

Dandelion and Burdock filled the room,
the yellow bottles kept in a cupboard,
caught, like a country afternoon, glowing
to the tick of a Spalding clock . . .
Your hands reddened in the industrial gloom,
but you wore an apron of spring daisies,
flowers to ignite the freeze of winter,
yellow sunshine on the drawn curtain.
There were no meadows outside your window.
You kept the cards in the same cupboard,
and hid them when the landlord visited,
or your brother, sanctimonious complainer,
treading the doorstep with his leather shoes,
not hearing the sound of your warm laughter,
the splash of streams on a September afternoon.

11. THE PAINTER'S DAUGHTER

Nightly you'd fetch the coal from the cellar
where your father painted watercolours,
straining his tired eyes in candle flame
to get that accuracy the family liked:
the crooked smile, geraniums in the yard.
Your hair was redder than flame. You hated
the hot dark, the scurrying squeak of rats.
You used candles, stumbling down the steps
until one night your hair caught fire
and your father leapt from the singeing dark,
smothering the flames with his bare arms.
Your hair was cropped close after that.
He never let you grow it long again.
Painted you once, a girl alone on moors,
her hair unruly in a sudden wind.

12. THE MURAL PAINTER

(For my grandfather)

i. Rituals

You packed us sandwiches at six o'clock,
your boots warming on the brass fender,
a swarm of starlings squabbling in the yard.
'You keep 'em fresh wi greaseproof paper.'
In the hall, the tick of the Spalding clock,
sunlight draining through nicotined curtains,
grandma, in the blue-tiled kitchen, singing.
You kept your tea hot in a corked bottle,
and these morning rituals I had never seen,
warmed at the ashes of the evening's fire,
talked into history like a family tree.
Then out into the street of black cobbles,
that dawn journey to Victoria Station
where the ice melted in your frozen workshop,
and your paints were stacked like a barn of corn.

ii. The Signwriter

Each winter morning was bright as steel,
terns in the sky like a painter's signature,
sunlight yellowing the frozen fields.
The bus dropped us at the end of a lane,
and we walked through grass heavy with frost,
the broken fragments kicked up like rainbows,
the breath of cattle smoking in the air.
'I painted murals before you were born,
oils and watercolours on pub walls,
summat unusual for folks to look at.'
I ate my sandwiches on a low stone wall,
and the brilliant scrawl of erratic terns
wheeled across the canvas towards Man Tor,
your voice a warm charcoal inside my mind,
your paints stacked tidily like a barn of corn.

13. SHELLING PEAS

Years after you preferred your own peas,
shelled into sunlight in a narrow yard
and rattled round the tin cullender
your father used for sorting out his brushes.
Your mother hated that. Folded her arms,
and glared at the polished doorstep,
her sightless eye glass with a fierce rage,
her flowered apron bright with April sun.
Just right, he claimed, the holes in that tin,
especially when you're working watercolour.
I bought frozen, shocking you with my lies.
They never taste the same. I think of you,
running down the yard, your brilliant hair
stopping their every argument,
shouting to help them shell the new peas.

The Imaginary Republic

(For Rachael)

You won't understand
Tizer and black puddings –
the thought of summer streams
dandelion-and-burdock brings –

Wizard and *Hotspur*
our penny-farthing literature . . . . .
but every Saturday morning,
I fetched licorice

and sherbert dips
from the corner off-licence,
and a farthing winked
in my hand like buttercups

in brilliant sunlight,
flames on a brass fender.
The imaginary republic
is our laughter,

seeing the tall snowmen
bow to their weeping wives,
the trams like red butterflies,
dancing on blue cables.

Sensation

(From Rimbaud's 'Sensation')

Blue evenings of summer grass
surround my passing.
The corn touches my feet.
In a dream, nothing in my mind,
I enjoy the sudden coolness.
Like a gypsy, softly pass.
Blue evenings,
the wind on my naked head.
Sensation of broken grass.

Hume's Fork

(Paris: 1978)

'For from my early reading of Faery Tales, & Genii &c &c – my
mind had been habituated to the Vast – & I never regarded my
senses in any way as the criteria of my belief.'

Coleridge

That horse butcher in Montmartre,
did he think you were crazy,
waving your Treatise in his face
and demanding Tabac? Tabac?
like a demented addict
from the Sorbonne,
souped up on literature and cafe?

I knew the exhilarating cold air,
cloudless September,
                        frost at midnight,
water tumbling down the streets at dawn,
the trees blind round Sacre Coeur.
I knew the absolute, baked heat
that drove the masses wild.

But not this passion:
Hume's fork despite a sky packed
with mackerel clouds –
cavorting planets on the run –
Paris seen from a railway carriage,
Calais to Gard du Nord,
cheap fare.

I breeze into your room
and find you reading Wolstonecraft:
'All this romantic crap,
bruised eyes, swollen lips,
cascades of luscious, auburn hair,
classic heroine stuff –
romantic idealism's dead and gone,
it's with religion in the grave.'

Your eyes blaze,
the love bites on your neck are blue,
cascades of auburn hair erupt . . . . .
romantic, idealist,
I dream my fantasies are true:

and read you the 'Ancient Mariner':
cloudless September,
                              frost at midnight,
walks by the River Seine at dawn . . . . .
familiar, absolute illusion:
the water under the bridges sighing,
flower-sellers offering French marigolds.
In our room, there is room
for manoeuvre,
but not this bright passion:
Paris from a second-hand *Michelin*,
Calais to Gard du Nord.
I hear the distant bells,
the clamour of Sacré Coeur,
welcoming another morning.
At the window, you see what I imagine:
Paris, smoking in its sun-thaw.

History

Trapped inside the window a fly sizzles
throughout your first political lecture,
distracting us from select committees
and examinations that must be passed
before we qualify for our own futures.
Too kind to commit murder at the beginning
of history, you ignore the fly and lose
the lesson to the mockers and fools,
then walk home with me through the rain,
your tweed jacket and brown leather patches
soaked in our dismal, northern weather,
your expensive brogues kicking up water.
'Things bought to last,' you smile,
'to withstand much use knocking on doors,
inviting people to vote for their conscience,
canvas an impossible, inevitable future.'
Things bought to last, like your quick smile,
refusal to deny the goodness of kings,
ridiculous, disrupting sense of humour . . .
Now I must walk on my own through rain,
splashing in pools of implacable water,
wearing my different, but expensive shoes.

Moving House

When we came here,
the woods were orange and burnt ochre,
an estate agent's dream
for quick selling,

the house safe
behind its larchwood fence,
surrounded by lawns
and trees that you said were cedar.

You always
knew more about trees than me.
You read all the brochures.
Such buying, you said, made sense.

And the selling
has been almost as easy,
what we paid for forgotten in the new move,
what we imagined difficult

like a swimmer
going back to swimming,
nervous on the edge of the pool,
then plunging through the cold water.

Guilt

The green earrings you wear
look Aztec, opaque,
mingling in your hair

like the tears you cried
when I left,
colouring the sky for years.

Getting up Early to Catch the Frost

(For Daniel)

Getting up early to catch the frost
I find it on the lawn ambushing a surprised cat,
rivetting itself into the frozen paths
to skid and delight milkman and postman –

invisible black frost dodging our threats,
creaking among the flower beds
that are graveyards of last year's colours,
cracking the helpless water in the watertub.

Along the paths, I fling my grenades of salt,
and they hiss like a flight of angry geese,
pecking at the ice with beaks of fury,
sizzling on the ground in snakes of hot sand.

The frost lashes back at me blindly.
My nose flinches. My eyes weep like watering cans.
My hands shrivel inside their furs.
The frost withers me with his crisp contempt.

Tractors and trees root to the earth in his grip.
Oak gateposts bend like tortured limbs,
rigid in their icicle handcuffs.
The cat on the larchwood fence somersaults.

I hurl even more bombs at the blackness.
They freeze, solid, in mid-air,
and fall like dead confetti to the ground.
I empty the container.

The lid clicks. The cardboard sticks to my hand.
I go back inside and load the fire with logs.
In the chimney the bricks protest
and the soot groans like a haunted train.

In the flames, blue faces snigger and leer.
The coal bucket clanks its metallic outcry,
expanding against ropes of contracting air.
The logs spit as they hit the fire.

And I spin in my terror.
I stare out of the rimed windows
through cathedrals and videos of ice.
I watch the spreading serials vibrate their victory anthem.

The frost grins inside.
Air thickens.
I jamb the letterbox and crouch for winter,
resigned to its drift through double glazing,

my arteries like motorways coursing their thin blood,
my limbs adjusting to immobility
as the cat whistles on the windowledge
and the soap operas make a freeze of the window.

In the garden,
a blackbird soprano sings.
A robin pecks at the icepond.
A thrush laughs.

Collecting Bottle Tops

Emptied into the yard, the sack of bottle tops
spun like silver fish on washed-down cobbles,
clattered and shimmered like a field of coins.
'There you are,' the publican grinned his pleasure,
rubbing his enormous, barrel-shifting arms,
flexing his tattooed fingers. 'I saved them for you.
Do with as you like. That's every beer we handle.'
Her arms buried in her spring-flowered apron,
my mother stood speechless at the kitchen door,
giggling on our polished, red-stone doorstep
at her yard suddenly full of revolving eyes,
spinning tops swimming round the red geraniums.
Behind curtains, a neighbour sniffed her derision.
When my father got home, he danced on cobbles,
racing across the yard in a drunken waltz,
cursing publicans and my deranged collections –
of stamps, of fish, and now steel marbles,
skidding beneath his feet like unspendable coins.
Delighted, the neighbour came to her door,
and asked if he was celebrating the new year,
six months early.

           My mother choked into her field of flowers,
a dream of buttercups filling her arms.
I watched it all from the bedroom window:
bottle tops swivelling in the moon's glare,
pennies for the eyes of the uncountable dead.
Behind a cloud, the moon courted a cold sun,
waiting for somebody to reverse the tides.
Down the backs, a trawler's siren whistled.
He must have taken them to the docks for drowning,
flinging them out beyond the lockpit pier,
grumbling about sacks that kept on floating,

like the sacks of vermin flung from the quays,
dosed with white powder to explode in darkness.
Amazed, a watchman asked him for tobacco,
thinking he was drunk with the midnight air,
shouting his fury at my mother's daftness.

I imagine the bottle tops floating out to sea,
cherry blossom petals with serrated rims,
a cargo of stars, dumped in the estuary,
drowned in the wake of a departing trawler.

                                    In the morning,
our yard was all cobbles,
and the neighbour swept dust into my eyes,
sneering at my mother's fancy apron.
'A publican's a strange friend for a boy,'
she smiled as I ran up the narrow passage,
urgent to catch the dawn tide.